WORDPLAY

Wild and Wacky Wordgames to Challenge Your Creativity

by Charles Thiesen and Deanna King

Cover Illustration by Angela Kamstra
Text Illustrations by Duane Barnhart

Meadowbrook

Distributed by Simon and Schuster
New York

Library of Congress Cataloging In Publication Data

Thiesen, Charles.
Wordplay

Summary: A collection of word games, literary exercises,
activities, and puzzles, including mysteries to solve and stories to finish.
1. Word games—Juvenile literature. [1. Word games. 2. Games.
3. Literary recreations.] I. King, Deanna. II. Title.
GV1507.W8T46 1986 793.73 86-16178
ISBN 0-88166-088-4 (pbk.)

Published by Meadowbrook, Inc., 18318 Minnetonka Boulevard, Deephaven, MN 55391.
Book Trade Distribution by Simon and Schuster, a division of Simon & Schuster, Inc.,
1230 Avenue of the Americas, New York, NY 10020.

S&S Ordering#:0-671-63099-7 (Priced)
          0-671-63231-0 (Unpriced)

10   9   8   7   6   5   4   3   2   1

Printed in the United States of America

Editor: Margaret Liddiard
Art Direction and Text Design:
Nancy MacLean Tuminelly
Cover Design: Mike Tuminelly
Cover Illustration: Angela Kamstra
Text Illustrations: Duane Barnhart
Keyline: Mike Tuminelly, Jill Rogers
Computer Graphics: Mike Tuminelly
Production: John Howard,
Nanci Jean Stoddard

Table of Contents

Introduction

Once upon a time words were invented. We wonder what that was like. Og and Zog sitting around the cave saying, "What will we call this?"

"Let's call it 'rock.'"

"OK, but then what will we call loud electric guitar music?"

Well, it probably wasn't like that. But we should be glad somebody invented words. If Og and Zog or somebody else hadn't invented words, not only wouldn't we be able to talk but we'd miss out on a lot of fun.

No words, no jokes. The chicken could still cross the road but no one could make up a joke about it.

No words, no word games. No "Hang Man" or "20 Questions."

No words, no riddles. Not only would newspapers not be read all over but no one could ask, "What's black and white and red (read) all over?" or "What fish has two knees?" (A two-knee fish, of course).

And, worst of all, no words, no "Wordplay."

Words are too much fun to do without and a lot of fun to do things with. That's what this book is all about. So when you've finished everything in this book; every "Hinky Pinky" and every "Here to There"; every last line of every poem and all the "Story Starters"; the whole "Wrong Answer Game" and all the crossword puzzles—when you've filled up every page of word fun in this book—DON'T STOP. Get some more paper and keep playing with words. There is a lot of word play here that you can do on your own: do more "Silly Sentences," make up your own "Hinky Pinkies," start your own stories. Keep having fun with words.

Now turn the page and start playing—with words.

May 1986
Charles Thiesen & Deanna King

Hinky Pinkies

How do you play HINKY PINKY?

First, you think up two rhyming words like "pretty kitty" or "flypaper skyscraper." Then you think up a definition. The definition for "pretty kitty" could be "a beautiful cat." "Pretty kitty" is a **hinky pinky** because both words have two syllables (sounds). The definition for "flypaper skyscraper" could be "a sticky building." It's a **hinkity pinkity** because "flypaper" and "skyscraper" both have three syllables. ("Fat cat" is a **hink pink** because both words have one syllable.)

Once you've thought up two rhyming words and the definition, ask a friend to guess your **hink pink**, **hinky pinky**, **hinkity pinkity** or whatever. It's great fun to play on long car trips!

(The answers are on page 114.)

1. A **hinky pinky** for happy Christmas greenery.

3. A **hink pink** for inexpensive grown-up lambs.

2. A cocoa colored evening dress—a **hink pink.**

4. A **hinky pinky** for sea movement.

5. What stinging insects kneel with—a **hink pink.**

_____

6. Bicycles owned by Michael—a **hink pink.**

_____

7. A **hink pink** for an actor's automobile.

_____

8. The lid on a soda bottle—a **hink pink.**

_____

9. A **hink pink** for a part of a sandwich that would be very heavy.

_____

10. When two baby buggies get hitched—a **hinky pinky.**

_____

11. A **hinky pinky** for someone who shouts in basements.

_____

12. A **hink pink** for haunted mail.

_____

13. What's a **hink pink** for a skin irritation caused by garbage?

_____

14. An imitation small horse—a **hinky pinky.**

_____

15. A **hinky pinky** for sweets on the beach.

_____

16. A pleased father—a **hinky pinky.**

_____

17. A **hink pink** for a sack for a joke.

_____

18. A wet light—a **hink pink.**

_____

19. An insect in your carpet—a **hink pink.**

_____

20. A **hinky pinky** for a spaceship charm.

_____

21. A bad-tempered person on a sofa—a **hink pink.**

_____

22. Playthings for young males—a **hink pink.**

_____

23. A **hink pink** for a funny story about a real soft drink.

_____

27. Jewelry for a bird's arm—a **hink pink.**

_____

28. A home for small rodents—a **hink pink.**

_____

24. Jam made for smearing on stomachs—a **hinky pinky**.

_____

29. A **hink pink** for a hopping reptile in the street.

_____

25. A **hinky pinky** for a cool William.

_____

26. A **hink pink** for trousers worn by little insects that like picnics.

_____

30. A **hink pink** for what long, slithery reptiles eat at birthday parties.

_____

Acrostic Poems

POEM

Ten put to paper
Or type on a page
Each holds
Much meaning for me

This is an **acrostic poem**. In an acrostic poem the first letters of the lines spell out a word or some words (usually a word that has something to do with the poem). **LIKE THIS:**

Round and juicy,
Every apple I eat is
Delicious and sweet.

Acrostic poems don't usually rhyme. Try some using these words:

F _____
R _____
U _____
I _____
T _____

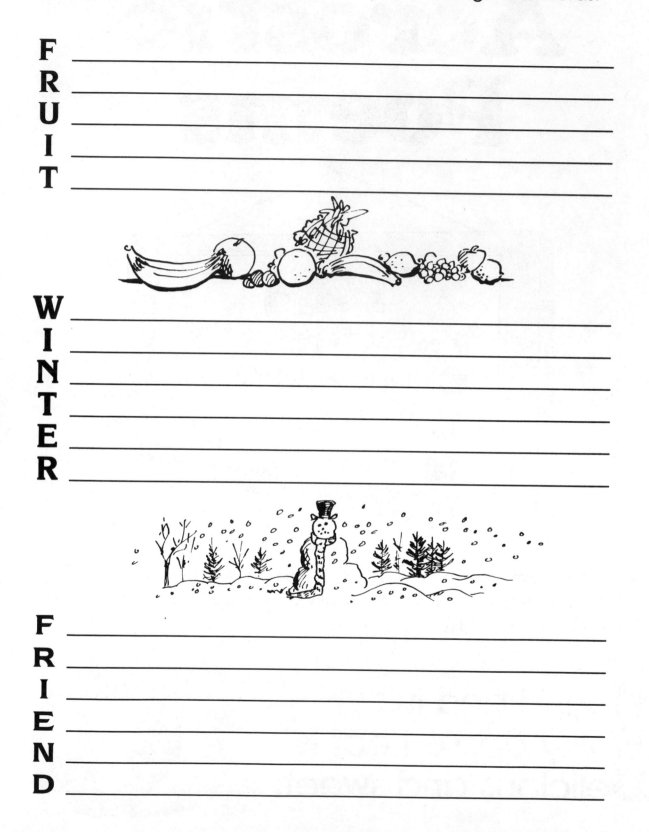

W _____
I _____
N _____
T _____
E _____
R _____

F _____
R _____
I _____
E _____
N _____
D _____

H O M E W O R K

_____
_____
_____
_____
_____
_____
_____
_____

F A T H E R

_____
_____
_____
_____
_____
_____

S I L L Y

_____
_____
_____
_____
_____

M
O
T
H
E
R

_____
_____
_____
_____
_____
_____

V
A
C
A
T
I
O
N

_____
_____
_____
_____
_____
_____
_____
_____

S
C
H
O
O
L

_____
_____
_____
_____
_____
_____

S _____

P _____

O _____

R _____

T _____

S _____

Now make up your own acrostics using any words you want.

_____

_____

_____

_____

_____

_____

_____

_____

_____

_____

_____

_____

_____

Story Starter #1:
THE CAVE

I stood at the mouth of the cave and tossed a rock in. Was that a growl or just an echo? I didn't want to go in but I had to. At least, I'd remembered to bring a flashlight . . .

(Why did you have to go in and what happened when you did?

Finish this story.)

KEEP OUT

THIS CHAPTER IS <u>SO</u> STRANGE

. . . **it might grow hair while you read this sentence and then go off for a shampoo.**

Now, that's a strange chapter.

Well, it isn't really **that** strange.

No. It hasn't gone off for a shampoo yet and I've been watching—so, why did you say it would?

Because it's fun to describe something by exaggerating. And it works better than just saying, "This is a really strange chapter." Here's another exaggerated description:

We went so fast we got back before we left.

My mom gave me so much ice cream that I could have put on a snorkel and gone for a swim in the bowl.

That's what I mean. That's a great exaggeration.

Try some of your own exaggerations here. We'll give you some things to describe, but when you've finished those, don't stop. Describe anything else you can think of.

You could keep on writing descriptions until the world ran out of trees to make your pencils.

She talks so loud . . .

_____

_____

His feet are so big . . .

_____

_____

The dog is so fierce . . .

_____

_____

My books are so heavy . . .

_____

_____

I have so much homework . . .

_____

_____

My bike is so fast . . .

_____

_____

It is so hot...

_____

_____

She is so dirty...

_____

_____

It tastes so bad...

_____

_____

She is so old...

_____

_____

It is so cold...

_____

_____

His hair is so long...

_____

_____

I'm so smart...

_____

_____

Now try some of your own . . .

_____

_____

_____

_____

_____

_____

_____

_____

_____

_____

_____

_____

_____

_____

_____

_____

_____

_____

_____

_____

THE CASE OF
The Science Class Code

"Hi," said Sherlock as he went into the fifth-grade science classroom.

"Bye," said Eric as he walked out the door and down the hall.

Melissa, James, and David were the only ones left in the room. "Where's he going?" Sherlock asked them.

"To the dentist," said James.

"He'll be back at lunch," added Melissa. "He's lucky he doesn't have to take the test today. Are you ready for it, Sherlock?"

Sherlock didn't answer. He was looking at his desk three rows away from where they were talking. He couldn't figure out what the piece of paper on it was. He knew he hadn't left it there.

"Sherlock," David said, "wake up."

"Oh. Sorry. Did any of you see somebody put that note on my desk?"

"I came in first and it wasn't there then. I didn't notice who put it there," said James.

"Me neither," said Melissa and David together.

Children were coming in one-by-one and in clumps of twos and threes. Sherlock wanted to see what the scrap of paper was but he had to sharpen his pencil and it was almost time for the bell.

Before he could get to his desk the bell rang and chairs scraped the tile floor as the class settled down. Mr. Cranmore, the teacher, walked up and down the rows of seats passing out the test. Sherlock rushed to his desk, sat down, and reached for the piece of paper.

"What's that?" asked Mr. Cranmore as he came up behind Sherlock's seat. Sherlock jumped.

"I don't know," said Sherlock. He handed the piece of paper to the teacher.

"It looks like some kind of code," said Mr. Cranmore. "Could these be the answers to the test?" He handed the piece of paper to Sherlock. It said:

CTATNEYLOLUMSETAATYSOOVCECREARTPMRYAHCOTUISCEETTOONDIAGYH

Everyone was staring at Sherlock. Mr. Cranmore turned to the class. "Who wrote this note to Sherlock?" he asked. No one spoke. The teacher turned back to Sherlock.

"I've never seen this code before, Mr. Cranmore, honest," said Sherlock.

"I don't think you're a cheater, Sherlock, but I have to have an explanation. I'm afraid if you can't explain this note to me by 3:00 this afternoon I'll have to keep you after school."

Sherlock felt sick. He didn't want to miss soccer practice at 3:15 but he had no idea how to explain the note.

"Sherlock, do you understand?" said Mr. Cranmore. "See me today at 3:00."

"Yes, Mr. Cranmore," said Sherlock. "Can I keep the note so I can try to figure it out?"

"I'll give it to you after the test," said the teacher, taking the note and walking up the aisle.

Sherlock looked down at his test and wrote his name at the top.

???

The bell rang, science class was over, and Sherlock was the first one out the door. He ran down the hall. "Walk please!" said a voice from down the hall.

Sheila, his sister, was coming out of her seventh-grade English class. "Sheila," said Sherlock, "you won't believe what—"

"We just got the weirdest case," Sheila interrupted. "For the last three mornings Larry has found a potato chip and a rose—"

"Sheila!" Sherlock shouted. "Listen to me. This is important."

"It better not be another case. Our detective business is booked." She walked toward her locker.

"I could be in **BIG** trouble," Sherlock said, hurrying to keep up. He told her about Mr. Cranmore and showed her the note.

Sheila looked at the note. "I don't know this code."

"You're kidding!" said Sherlock. "Now what'll I do?"

"Do you think you can find out who sent it?"

"Mr. Cranmore asked the class but no one admitted it. I don't know what else I can do."

"Well, I'll go through the box of codes and see if I can find this one." They'd reached her locker where she opened the door and took out an old cigar box with CODES written on the top.

"What if it really is the test answers? Then what'll I do?"

"Then you really better find out who sent it. Think about what happened in class and see if you can come up with any clues. I mean, someone must have sent it."

"I know, I know," Sherlock sighed.

"Hey, don't worry. We'll figure it out. We always have before. . . . Well, almost always."

"Oh, great."

"I'll meet you at lunch," Sheila said. She stuck the code box under her arm and ran off down the hall.

"Walk please," called an adult voice from the other end of the hall. She slowed down.

???

"Quiet in the hot lunch line," shouted Mrs. Pratt, the principal.

Sherlock went up to her. "Have you seen my sister Sheila?"

"What?" yelled Mrs. Pratt.

"HAVE YOU SEEN—"

"You'll have to shout louder, Sherlock." He could barely hear her shouting back.

"Never mind, I see her." Mrs. Pratt still didn't know what he said but she turned her attention to another problem when he walked away.

Sheila was sitting at one of the tables with benches attached. She was staring at the code box wedged in between a carton of milk and a still-wrapped sandwich.

"Hi," said Sherlock.

"Forget it," said Sheila, "I can't find the code."

"You're kidding."

"No. I looked through them all," she held up a fist full of different-sized pieces of paper. "None of them fit the code in your note."

"What am I going to do now? I'll miss soccer practice and who knows what else Mr. Cranmore will do to me if he thinks I was cheating." He picked up the code box, turned it upside down, and shook it. The top dropped open and a tattered piece of paper fluttered onto the table. "Look Sheila, there's one more code."

"That WAS a code until Dr. Watson (our dog) chewed on it last year when he was still a puppy. It's really yucky and impossible to read. Throw it out."

Sherlock was peering closely at the scrap of code. "Wait a minute. I can make out some of it. It says: 'Divide...half...space...letter.'"

"I remember it!" shouted Sheila.

"Quiet please," yelled a teacher from the next aisle.

"Last year," Sheila said, "some fourth-grade boys brought us a really hard code to break. That's the solution. To put something in the code you divide the message in half and put each letter of the second half in between the letters of the first half. So to decode it you take the first letter, skip a letter, take the next letter, skip a letter, and so on through the message. Then you take the letters you skipped."

"I don't understand."

"Well, let's put something in the code. How about 'I like you.'"

"Okay."

"That has eight letters so we write out the first four with spaces in between like this." She took a piece of paper and wrote:

I___L___I___K___

"Then we write the last four letters in the spaces like this." She wrote:

I_E_L_Y_I_O_K_U

I get it," said Sherlock. "Let me put something in code and see how you decode it." He wrote:

D V E E T S E D C E T S I K

Sheila took the paper and wrote:

D E T E C T I

"Is that right so far?" she asked.

"Yes, but how did you do it?"

"I started with the D and skipped the V and wrote the E and skipped the next E and so on. Now I'll write the letters I skipped." When she was finished the message looked like this:

D E T E C T I V E S D E S K

"It says 'Detective's Desk,'" she said. "That's us. Do you think we can decode your message now?" She handed him the paper with the message on it. The message said:

CTATNEYLOLUMSETAATYSOOVCECREARTPMRYAHCOT-UISCEETTOONDIAGYH

(Try solving this yourself. The solution is on page 114. Then you can use this code to write your own secret messages.)

"Sure. Easy," said Sherlock.

"We only have a few minutes to the bell," Sheila said.

Sherlock ripped two pages from Sheila's notebook and handed one to her. They started writing.

It didn't take them long to figure it out. Sheila handed hers to Sherlock. "Is this what yours says?"

"Yes. It's a nice message. But it's not signed so I don't know who to give the answer to."

"But at least you can get out of trouble with Mr. Cranmore."

"Right. That's a relief. But I wish I knew who sent it."

"Why don't we each try to figure it before soccer," said Sheila.

"But how do we do that?"

"I'll bet I can. What happened in science class today?"

"I get it," said Sherlock. "The old 'looking-for-clues' trick."

"Just tell me the facts."

"When I got to science class, Eric was just leaving to go to the dentist and Melissa, James, and David were the only ones in the room. I talked to them for a few minutes, then I saw the note on my desk. James told me that it hadn't been there when he came in—"

"That's enough," Sheila interrupted and started writing in the back cover of her notebook.

"What are you writing?"

"The name of the mystery note writer."

"I don't believe it," Sherlock said. "You know already?"

"It's obvious." Sheila was smiling a smug smile that made Sherlock want to figure it out himself.

He said, "Don't tell me how you figured it out. I want to do it myself. After I see Mr. Cranmore I'll meet you at the swings and I'll bet I know who wrote the note by then."

The lunch bell rang. Sheila put the codes back into the box and closed it. She put her uneaten sandwich back in its bag.

"I've got to run," she said. "Throw this away for me?" She held up her empty milk carton.

Sherlock didn't move. "Please, Sherlock, I'll be late for class." Sherlock stared into space.

"Sherlock, why are you staring!"

"Oh," Sherlock said, noticing Sheila. "I just got an idea how to find the sender."

"Good," said Sheila. She shoved the empty milk carton into his hands and ran off. "See you at the swings," she shouted over her shoulder.

"Please walk," Mrs Pratt called from the other side of the lunchroom.

???

When Sherlock got to the school playground, Sheila was already on the swings and Eric was swinging alongside. They were pumping hard and fast.

"Eric!" Sherlock yelled, "you sent me the note."

Eric nodded, dragged his feet under his swing and slowed to a stop.

"Sheila, watch out, you're losing your notebook," Eric said.

Her yellow notebook slipped from under her arm and dropped in the dust by the swing. Sherlock picked it up while she slowed the swing. He turned to the back of the notebook. "It says 'Eric,'" Sherlock said. "So we both got it. Right, Eric?"

"Right. But how did you know since I forgot to sign my note?"

Sheila and Sherlock both started to talk at once. Then they stopped and both said, "You first," together. They couldn't stop laughing.

Finally Sherlock said, "You figured it out first so you tell it first."

"Okay. I knew it had to be Eric because if the sender had been in the room when Mr. Cranmore found the note, he would have admitted writing it so you wouldn't get in trouble. Don't you think?"

"Yes," said Sherlock. "The sender was a friend."

"Well, then it had to be Eric because he was the only one who could have put the note on your desk who wasn't there to say he wrote it."

"Of course," said Eric. "That makes sense. Sorry I almost got you in trouble, Sherlock."

"But how did *you* figure it out, Sherlock?" Sheila asked.

"Oh, I didn't. I just wrote a note in that code and put it in the lockers of who could have sent my note: James, Melissa, David, and Eric."

"What did it say?"

Eric said, "Mine said, 'Meet me at the swings after school.' And Sherlock remembered to sign it." He blushed.

"Right. They all said that. Whoever sent the note would know the code and would come here. So when I saw Eric I knew it was him."

"Good detecting, Sherlock," said his big sister.

"You too," he said.

Eric jumped. "Well, Sherlock, what's your answer?"

"I have to ask my mom."

"Okay, let's go over to your house after soccer practice."

"Okay. And we'd better hurry if we're going to get to practice on time." They ran out of the playground shouting goodbye to Sheila.

"Bye," she shouted back, and then she opened the cover of her notebook. At the top it said "CASES." The last entry read:

The Case of the Science Class Code

Next to it she wrote "**SOLVED.**"

THE END

Story Starter #2:
A LONG JOURNEY

When we saw it in the field we thought it was a make-believe flying saucer. Maybe someone was making a movie. We had to see what it looked like so we went inside. I was fooling around and I touched a button on the control panel. Then things started to happen. . .

(What started to happen? Who was with you? Finish the story.)

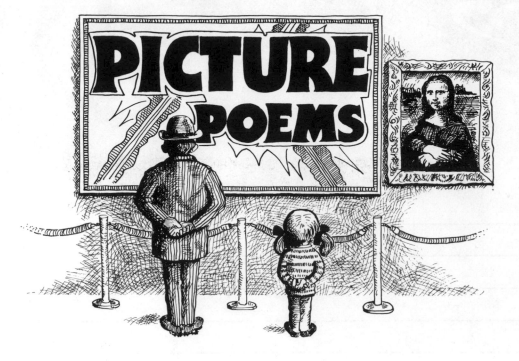

A Picture Poem is a poem that looks like what it is about.

It's shaped or drawn or colored so that it reminds you of what it is talking about, even before you read it. Look at the poems below.

Mix-Up

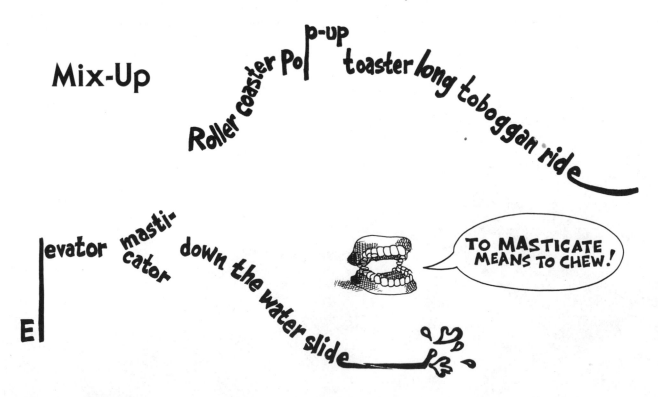

Roller coaster Po**p-up** toaster long toboggan ride

Elevator masti-cator down the water slide

TO MASTICATE MEANS TO CHEW!

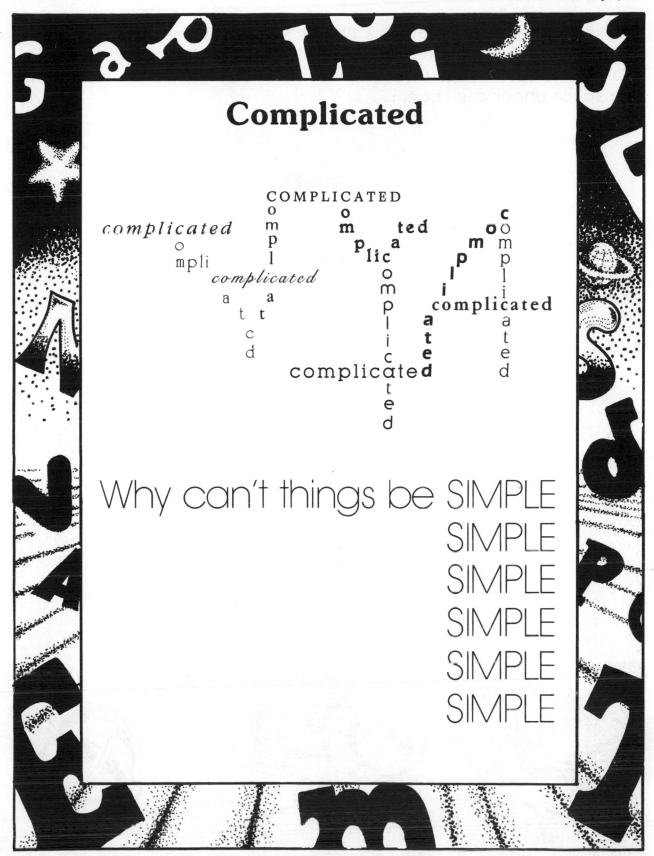

Complicated

Why can't things be SIMPLE
SIMPLE
SIMPLE
SIMPLE
SIMPLE
SIMPLE

Rhyming isn't important in a **Picture Poem**. What is important is what the poem looks like. Make your own **Picture Poems** with crayons, markers or anything you want. You can make up the poem yourself in the space under each poem...

Top
A top spins
round and round
until it wobbles
and stops.

Merry-Go-Round

The horses on the merry-go-round
Go up and down and up and down
And round and round until they stop
And some are up and some are down
And some stay in-between.

Bounce

I bounce my ball a little higher
Every time I bounce it. O!
And if I miss
It bounces, bounces,
Lower, lower, every bounce.

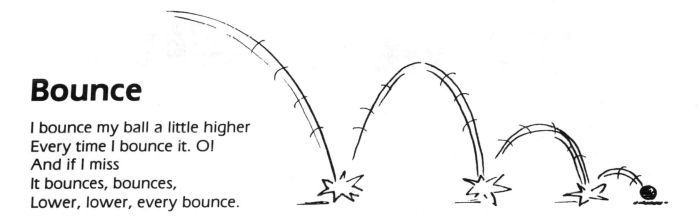

Tightrope

Walking a tightrope is tricky
Take one false step and
down you go
until you hit the net

Marching

Left Right
Left Right
Left Right
Marching
Marching
Left Right
Left Right
Marching Marching
Very Tired
Left Right
Left

silly sentences

Silly sentences sound so:
super...sassy...satisfying...smart...superior...soothing..

Soothing!?

Sure, why not? It begins with an 's' and that's all
that matters. Anyway, as I was saying: Silly
Sentences sound so stupid, sickening, and scrat-
chy. Start some Silly Sentences soon.

What's that all about?

That's a Silly Sentence. So is this: Tiny
Tina took ten tomatoes to toss toward Tall
Tim. Tomatoes Tim turned into tamales.

That's two sentences and, besides, 'into'
doesn't start with a 'T'.

So what?

Try making up some of your own Silly Sentences. Just start most of the words with the same sound. Here's some space and some letters to start with:

S _____

_____

G _____

_____

H _____

_____

P _____

_____

M _____

_____

T _____

_____

Now try writing some **Silly Sentences** of your own, using any letter you want.

_____

_____

_____

_____

_____

_____

_____

_____

_____

THE CASE OF
The Keyless Code

Sherlock ran after the paper as it blew down the sidewalk. He heard a voice behind him call, ''Hey, Sherlock!'' but he kept running. He didn't stop until the paper blew into a large puddle in the street and settled down into the brown water. He turned around then and saw William coming up beside him.

''Was that important?'' William asked.

''It was my math homework. I don't know what I'll tell Ms. Goldstein.''

Sheila, Sherlock's big sister, had just run up. ''Tell her the truth,'' she said, puffing, a little out of breath. ''Your homework blew into a puddle.''

"She'll never believe me. I wouldn't believe me." He stood and stared at the paper, barely visible through the murky water. "But I'm not going in there to get it."

"Sherlock," said William.

Sherlock just looked at the puddle.

"Sherlock," he said again, but when Sherlock didn't move, William turned to Sheila.

"Sheila, I have a mystery for you two. It's a code." He took his school pack off his back, took a smudged envelope out of it, and handed it to Sheila. "Thomas gave this to me on his way out of town with his parents."

Sherlock turned around, "You mean Thomas gets to miss school today?"

"That's right."

"Then he doesn't have to hand in any math homework. Lucky him."

Sheila had taken the note out of the envelope and was looking at it. "Don't you have the key to the code?" she asked.

"No. That's the problem."

"Wait a minute," said Sherlock, "let me see that." Sheila handed him the envelope. He looked closely at it, then said, "I have it. The key is in the envelope."

"What do you mean, Sherlock?" Sheila asked.

"Look," he said, "it says so right here." He held up the envelope. On the outside was written: "THE KEY IS INSIDE THE ENVELOPE." Sheila and Sherlock both looked at William.

"Come on you two," William said, "don't you think I saw that? There wasn't anything inside the envelope but the code, honest."

Sherlock turned the envelope over and shook it but nothing came out.

"Can you work on it?" asked William.

"Sure," said Sheila, "I think we can get to it next week."

"Oh no! I was hoping you could solve it by the end of school today." William looked very upset.

"What's the matter, William?" asked Sherlock.

"I'm supposed to go on a bike trip with my dad tomorrow and my bike is missing. I think it was stolen."

"But what does that have to do with this code?" Sheila asked.

"Thomas said that he thought he knew who had taken it but he didn't want to tell me until he was sure. He must have found out and the answer is in the code. I just wish he'd remembered to put the key in the envelope."

The three children started toward school. Sherlock picked up a rock and turned back and threw it into the puddle. It made a big, messy splash.

"Feel better?" asked Sheila.

Sherlock nodded.

"Where did you leave your bike last?" Sheila asked William.

"I rode it home after school yesterday and left it in front of my house. Then I played ball with Chris and Joe down the street. It started raining so I went home and when I got there my bike was gone."

They got to school just as the bell rang. "Let's meet at lunch," said Sheila as they hurried into the front door with hundreds of other children.

???

The lunchroom was packed and noisy. Sherlock and Sheila sat on a bench and leaned their elbows on the table. William stood behind them looking over their shoulders at the note on the table. Three lunch bags sat unopened next to the piece of paper.

"This is going to be hard," said Sheila.

They all looked at the note:

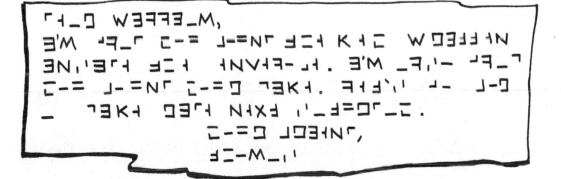

"Well, let's figure this out," Sheila said and got a pad and pencil from the pile of books alongside her on the bench.

Sherlock pointed at the first line. "I'll bet this says, 'Dear William.'"

"That must be it," said Sheila. "Look, there's a 'W' and an 'M' in the right place."

"So maybe the last line says, 'Yours truly, Thomas,'" Sherlock said.

"But those words don't have the right number of letters," said Sheila.

William said, "He usually signs his letters, 'Your friend, Thomas.'"

"That does have the right number of letters. That's great," said Sheila. "It gives us lots of letters and we can match them up with more of the message."

They put the letters they knew by the words they went with, like this:

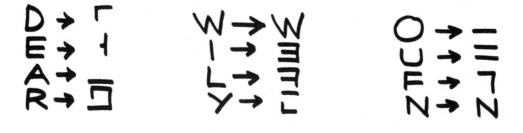

And then they made a list of letters they knew, like this:

Using that they decoded the first sentence of the message. This is what Sheila wrote:

(I'M __ LAD YOU FOUND THE KEY WRITTEN INSIDE THE EN__ELOPE.)

William looked at it and said, "That last word must be envelope so it must say 'I'm *glad* you found the key written inside the *envelope*.'"

"But we looked inside the envelope," Sherlock said.

"Let me see it again," said Sheila. She took the envelope and carefully tore it apart along the seams. There, written on the inside of the envelope, was this message:

(MOST LETTERS CAN BE MADE FROM PARTS OF THIS SHAPE:

TO PUT A LETTER IN CODE DRAW IT SO THAT IT FITS THE SHAPE, LIKE THIS:

A = ☐   B = ☐

THEN TAKE THE PART OF THE SHAPE NOT USED IN THE LETTER, LIKE THIS:

THE LETTERS THAT DON'T FIT, LIKE K, W, M, AND V, I JUST WRITE OUT.)

Sheila said, "It's your message, William. Why don't you figure it out?"

(Figure it out yourself. The answer is on page 114.)

When William was finished they were all a little surprised.

"Why did Thomas say you found your bike?" asked Sherlock suspiciously.

"Honest, Sherlock, I don't know. I haven't found my bike and this message doesn't really help me at all."

"Maybe it does," said Sheila. "We'll go over to Thomas's house and try to figure out why he thinks you found your bike. Meet us after school, William."

???

Thomas's house was almost across the street from William's. As they passed William's house he said, "See? There's my house and I left my bike right in front and it's not there."

Sheila walked right up to Thomas's front door. The boys followed her. "Where would Thomas have been when he wrote the note?" she asked William.

"Well, sometimes he wrote up in that tree." William pointed at a big tree in the front yard.

Sheila walked over to the tree and climbed up about ten feet. Then she climbed down. "I've solved it," she said and led the two boys across the street to William's house. She walked to the side of the house and pulled a bicycle out from behind two garbage cans that sat under a protective shed attached to the side of the house.

"You couldn't see the bike from the ground," said Sheila, "but I saw it from the tree. Thomas must have seen it when he was writing you the note, and since it was by your house he thought you found it."

"But how did it get there?" William asked.

Sherlock said, "I've got an idea. You said it was raining when you came back home. Maybe someone put your bike in there to keep it dry as a favor and didn't know you wouldn't be able to see it."

"Right," said Sheila. "If it was a grown-up they could probably see it from the street and didn't know that you couldn't. I wonder who did it?"

"We don't have to figure that out, too, do we, Sheila?" asked Sherlock.

"I don't think so," she said. "I'd say this case is closed. Right, William?"

"I'm just glad I got my bike back. Thanks a lot."

Sherlock and Sheila walked down the path to the street.

"We're a pretty good team," said Sherlock.

"The best," said Sheila. She linked arms with her brother and they walked toward home.

THE END

Story Starter #3:
ONE WISH

Of course I pulled the cork from the bottle when I found it on the beach. Wouldn't you? But the genie that popped out was not what I expected. It only offered me one wish. I was angry. "One wish!" I shouted. "That's not fair." But the genie wouldn't change its mind. So I had to think about my wish very carefully.

(What did you wish and what happened then? Finish the story.)

_____

_____

_____

_____

_____

_____

_____

_____

_____

ADLIBS

Adlibs are word __games__ . All you have to do to
Noun

__play__ Adlibs is fill in the __blanks__ in the first section
Verb   Noun

with the kind of word it asks for. When you're done you put those

words in the blanks in the story and see how

__well__ they fit.
Adverb

We give you lists of __good__ nouns, adjectives, and
Adjective

adverbs to make it easier but you don't have to use ours. It's more

fun to __think__ up your own.
Verb

The other blanks, like ''an animal'' or ''a liquid,'' are easy to fill

so we won't give you any examples.

The wonderful thing about Adlibs is that when they're done
they're not supposed to make sense.

Try filling in these blanks. (You'll find a word list on the next page in case you need some help thinking up words.)

ADJECTIVE: _____

NOUN: _____

NOUN: _____

NOUN: _____

KIND OF ANIMAL: _____

ADVERB: _____

NOUN: _____

ADJECTIVE: _____

ADVERB: _____

NOUN: _____

PLURAL NOUN: _____

(*plural* means more than one)

ADVERB: _____

NOUN: _____

NOUN: _____

ADJECTIVE: _____

ADJECTIVE: _____

LIQUID: _____

NOUN: _____

KIND OF ANIMAL: _____

NOUN: _____

NOUN: _____

ADJECTIVE: _____

NOUN: _____

NOUN: _____

NOUN: _____

EXCLAMATION: _____

(like "Oh my!" or "Dagnabbit!")

ADJECTIVE: _____

KIND OF ANIMAL: _____

ANIMAL SOUND: _____

Now read this story using the words from your list.

THE CASE OF THE

_____ _____
Adjective   Noun

Sheila and Sherlock sat on their _____ outside their
                                              Noun

_____ watching Dr. Watson (their _____) playing
Noun   Kind of animal

_____ with a _____. They were feeling very
Adverb   Noun

_____ because they were working on a case. _____
Adjective   Adverb

they decided to go to the scene of the _____. They got on their
Noun

_____ and rode _____ down the _____ to the
Plural noun   Adverb   Noun

haunted _____.
Noun

When they got there it was very _____. They were
Adjective

_____ so they decided to have a drink of _____ and
Adjective   Liquid

then they sat on a _____ to think. Dr. Watson (their
Noun

_____) ran up and licked Sheila on her _____.
Kind of animal   Noun

Suddenly Sheila said, "I've got it. The _____ must have hid
Noun

the _____ _____ under the _____. Now all we
   Adjective   Noun   Noun

have to do is tell the police and they'll give us a _____."
                                                     Noun

"_____ Sheila, that's _____, said Sherlock. "I don't
Exclamation   Adjective

know how you do it."

Dr. Watson (their _____) said "_____." **THE END**
                Kind of animal   Animal noise

Here are some ideas for words:

NOUNS*	ADJECTIVES*	ADVERBS*
toy	old	slowly
box	young	quickly
head	slippery	heavily
carrot	smooth	lightly
baby	hot	cleverly
wall	cold	stupidly
nut	high	healthily
window	low	well
car	nice	poorly
shirt	mean	badly
hairpin	bad	nimbly
painting	good	gracefully
flower	happy	clumsily
ring	sad	thankfully
finger	bumpy	hopefully
bird	rough	daintily
meat	fast	smartly
chicken	slow	curiously
computer	tender	piercingly
hammer	tough	loudly
tree	light	softly
neck	square	quietly
pencil	round	painfully
lunch box	straight	dangerously
apple	bouncy	safely
store	steady	carefully
pill	boring	noisily
hillside	exciting	smoothly
bicycle	interesting	roughly
hair	clear	kindly
pillow	cloudy	knowingly
nest	rainy	

*A **noun** is a person, place, or thing.

*An **adjective** describes a noun.

*An **adverb** describes a verb. Verbs are "action" words, and adverbs describe **how** they are done.

If you like **Adlibs** you can get *Madlibs* in bookstores. *Madlibs* are just like **Adlibs**. They are published by Price/Stern/Sloan.

HERE TO THERE

How do you get from **BLOCK** to **CREAM**? It's easy if you're playing **Here to There**. You start with a word—like **BLOCK**. Then, by changing one letter at a time you turn it into another word—like **CREAM**.

BLOCK change the **B** to **C** and get

CLOCK change the second **C** to **A** and get

CLOAK change the **L** to **R** and get

CROAK change the **O** to **E** and get

CREAK change the **K** to **M** and wind up with

CREAM

The only other rule is that each time you change a letter you have to make a new real word. Try these. We'll give you some hints.

J O L L Y

— — — — —   (Christmas greenery)

— — — — —   (steep, but not mountainous)

— — — — —   (small mountains)

— — — — —   (knife handles)

H I N T S

This time we won't give you any hints but we will tell you which letter to change each time.

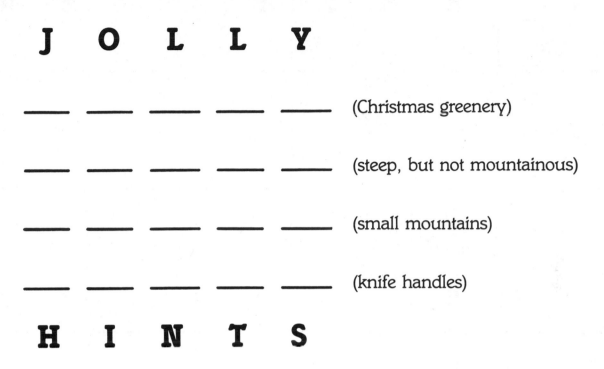

P R A N K

B L E E D

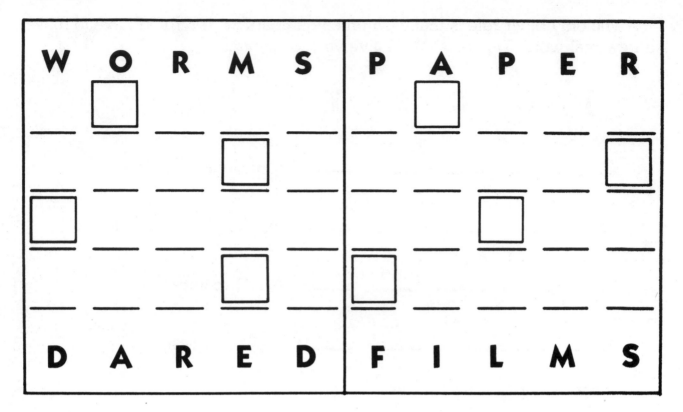

Now use these clues to get from **Here to There**

D R I N K

_____ _____ _____ _____ _____ what you did with water

_____ _____ _____ _____ _____ a trick

_____ _____ _____ _____ _____ wooden board

_____ _____ _____ _____ _____ you fly one

P L A T E

We won't give you any clues for this one (except this picture).

P L A N T

— — — — —

— — — — —

— — — — —

— — — — —

B R I N K

F L O C K

□ — — — —

— □ — — —

— — □ — —

— — — □ —

B R A N D

B I K E R

— □ — — —

— — — — □

— — □ — —

— — — □ —

T A S K S

(See solutions, page 115)

The End of Poetry

Sometimes the hardest thing about writing a poem is writing the first line. Sometimes the easiest thing about writing a poem is writing the last line.

Take limericks. The last line of a limerick is supposed to rhyme with the first two, like this:

A Zambian princess, I've heard,
Who'd just learned a new English word
Said, "It cannot be so
What you call that. Oh, no!
Not 'Butter Fly'—why that's absurd."

"ABSURD" MEANS THE SAME AS "RIDICULOUS," BUT "RIDICULOUS" DOESN'T RHYME WITH "WORD."

Try writing last lines for these. We'll give you hints about some words that rhyme in some of them (but you don't have to use our ideas).

YOU'D B-B-B-B-BUTTER NOT EAT THAT!

A teacher who'd taught in Calcutta
While dining was once heard to mutter,
"I've had to eat ants
And frightening plants

_____."

Said a sitter, one day, to a child,
"Your behavior is not very mild.
You are making me frown,
Drink warm milk and calm down,

_____." "

Two landlords were talking in Trent.
"How much do you charge for your rent?"
"Ten dollars a day
And more if they stay

_____." "

A grandma said to her grandson,
"My boy, I forbid you to run."
"It's so tempting," he said.
And he grabbed her and sped.

_____.

In a castle that had a deep moat
Lived a chicken, a duck, and a goat.
When they had to go out
To wander about

_____.

A diner with very sore feet
Who stood up in order to eat
Said with a frown,
"I'd sure like to sit down

_____." "

Said the cow to the horse, "Let's elope."
Said the horse to the cow, "Thank you, nope.
I won't marry a cow,
At least not right now

_____." "

In Oshkosh, Wisconsin, it's said,
Lived a man who once buttered his head.
When asked why he had
He looked very sad

_____.

A turtle named Archibald Hall
Said, "I wish that I wasn't so small."
"You're taller than I,"
Said an ant with a sigh.

_____.

Here are some poems that rhyme but aren't limericks.

My Pocket

"What's in your pocket?" said Mother to me.
"Some fuzz, a bent nail, a pebble and gee...
Three rubber bands and a bright, shiny stone

_____. "

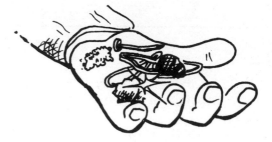

Too Close to Supper

Much too close to suppertime I sailed out to sea.
There I caught a mermaid who said she'd give to me
Anything I wanted, whatever I might wish,

_____.

Math

I don't much like to multiply eight times seventy-three.
Every time I do it, it comes out differently.
I'd much rather do three times three or one times ninety-two.

_____.

And adding five plus nine plus seven plus twelve plus fifty-four
Plus twenty-nine plus ninety-one is really such a bore.
It's not that I have trouble, it's as easy as can be

_____.

Painting

I'd paint my bedroom orange if I had the chance,
And then when I was finished I'd do a little dance,
Then I'd paint the living room in fire-engine red

_____ .

The kitchen should be purple, I think that's very nice,
And if I had a laundry room I'd paint it blue as ice.
When I'd finished painting rooms I'd wallpaper the door

_____ .

NO, I'M NOT HURT, BUT I SURE AM <u>ANGRY!</u>

The Ice

The ice is slippery, I go slow
But tumble, tumble, down I go.
I don't get hurt, it isn't bad

_____ .

What's It For?

Tissues are for runny noses.
Band-Aids are for cuts.
Vases are for long-stemmed roses.

_____ .

Highways are for cars and trucks.
Airports are for planes.
Bad weather is good for ducks.

_____ .

How Come

How come homework is so boring
And playing games is fun,
And having lots of friends is better

_____ ?

How come it's light in the morning
And dark when I go to bed?
How come feet are at the bottom

_____ ?

Butterfly High

Butterfly, high,
What does it see?
Butterfly, high,
The ground and me.
Butterfly, high,
Where does it go?
Butterfly, high,

_____ .

Butterfly, high,
Where does it look?
Butterfly, high,

_____ .

Here are some poems without last lines. You can write anything you want. It can rhyme, but it doesn't have to.

The Sun
The sun doesn't bounce,
It sits still in the sky.
My rubber ball,

_____.

Tickle
I love to be tickled.
I love to laugh, to bubble, to giggle
And roll on the floor like a

_____.

I love to be tickled.
I love to gasp 'cause the world seems so funny,
Then crawl away under the table and

_____.

If I
If I walk barefoot in the snow,
My feet will get cold, my toes will freeze.
If I wear mittens in summer,
My hands will get warm and sweaty and itchy.
If I open my eyes in bed at night,
I won't get to sleep for a long, long time.

_____.

_____.

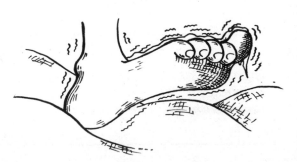

Night
When I go to bed at night,
The sky is dark and still.
Thoughts are running round my brain,

Like _____.

When I go to bed at night,
The house is very quiet.
I start to dream before I know it,

And _____.

Smells
My nose is twitching.
Something's cooking.
It pulls me to the kitchen.
It sniffs around with me behind it.

_____.

Wild Child
I am a child,
Wild and strong.
Treat me right,

Grass
I like grass.
If I were a cow I'd eat it.
I like grass.
If I were a bug I'd live in it.
I like grass.

_____.

_____.

In the next poem add as much or as little as you like:

Meals
Pizza for breakfast,
Candy for lunch,
Popcorn for supper,

_____.

_____.

_____.

_____.

_____.

_____.

Branching Stories

To read a branching story just choose what you want to have happen (a. or b.) then go to the box that the **Go to** tells you to go to and make your next choice. For example, if you want to:

a. read this chapter. (Go to 1.)
b. skip this chapter. (Go to the next chapter.)

---

1. Once there was a young writer who:
 a. wrote a branching story. (Go to 2.)
 b. didn't write a branching story. (Go to 18.)

5. The trees weren't very interesting, so the writer went home to write the story. (Go to 18.)

---

2. It was a story about an adventure in
 a. the jungle. (Go to 3.)
 b. the schoolyard. (Go to 8.)

6. And was eaten. (Go to 18.)

---

3. In order to write a story about the jungle the writer went to Africa to do research and went for a walk and came face to face with:
 a. a tiger. (Go to 4.)
 b. a kitten. (Go to 7.)

7. "A kitten?" said the writer, "this isn't much of a jungle. I'm going home." And the writer went home. (Go to 18.)

---

4. "A tiger!" said the writer, "this is a real jungle." The writer:
 a. decided to learn more and went right up to the tiger to see what it was really like. (Go to 6.)
 b. thought that it wasn't safe to get too close to the tiger and decided to learn more about the trees in the distance. (Go to 5.)

8. To research the story, the writer went to the schoolyard to see what was going on.
 a. There was a softball game, a basketball game, and some children hanging out talking. (Go to 9.)
 b. There was a softball game, a basketball game, and a group of children standing around a very large hole in the center of the schoolyard. (Go to 10.)

9. This didn't seem to be an interesting story, so the writer decided to:
   a. write about a jungle. (Go to 3.)
   b. go home and do some homework. (Go to 18.)

10. Looking over the edge of the hole the writer:
   a. saw a flying saucer at the bottom. (Go to 11.)
   b. fell three feet into the hole and got scraped knees and decided to go home. (Go to 18.)

11. The flying saucer:
   a. was made out of papier mache and sticks and was only three feet wide. It had been made by the seventh grade for their play. (Go to 12.)
   b. began to glow and slowly rose out of the hole until it was so high it disappeared. (Go to 13.)

12. But how had it gotten in the hole and what had made the hole?
   a. The writer didn't care. (Go to 9.)
   b. The writer decided to find out. (Go to 13.)

13. The writer:
   a. asked the children standing around the hole if any of them knew anything. (Go to 14.)
   b. went to buy a newspaper to see if there was a story about the hole. (Go to 17.)

14. The children:
   a. said they didn't know anything, so the writer decided to write a different story.(Go to 2.)
   b. told the writer everything they knew. (Go to 15.)

15. **a.** It seemed that during the night the ground beneath the playground had collapsed because of a broken water pipe. When the seventh graders were carrying their flying saucer from the classroom to the auditorium they almost fell into the hole and dropped the saucer in. (Go to 18.)
   b. The story was very complicated and involved a gang of criminals who had done some very mean things. (Go to 16.)

16. The writer wrote the story and the criminals were punished and the writer received a big reward. (Go to 18.)

17. There wasn't. (Go to 18.)

18. **THE END**

Now try writing your own **Branching story** in these boxes.

You can't call these lies because they don't fool anybody. They're just wrong answers. Some people call them **Tall Tales.** But whatever you call them they're fun to make up.

One thing about wrong answers though, the longer they are, the better. The more nonsense you can come up with to answer the simplest question, the more fun it is.

Try some wrong answers to these questions or make up your own questions and answer them. If the answer is too long for the space, use another piece of paper.

What's your name?

_____

_____

_____

Where do you live?

_____

_____

_____

What do you eat?

_____

_____

_____

What's your favorite food?

_____

_____

_____

What do you want to be when you grow up?

_____

_____

_____

What do you look like?

_____

_____

_____

What do you do all day?

_____

_____

_____

Where do you sleep?

_____

_____

_____

What does your house look like?

_____

_____

_____

What grows in your garden?

_____

_____

_____

Where do you go for vacation?

_____

_____

_____

What do you do on weekends?

_____

_____

_____

What movies are you starring in right now?

_____

_____

_____

What are you famous for?

_____

_____

_____

Have you ever been on TV?

_____

_____

_____

What do you see from your bedroom window?

_____

_____

_____

What did you get for your last birthday?

_____

_____

_____

Now try some of your own.

_____

_____

_____

_____

_____

_____

_____

_____

_____

_____

_____

_____

_____

_____

_____

_____

_____

_____

_____

Story Starter #4:
RULER OF THE SCHOOL

When all of the votes had been counted I was elected Ruler of the School for a day. I could do anything I wanted...anything at all. I knew exactly what to do. **(Oh did you? Exactly what did you do? Finish the story.)**

_____

_____

_____

_____

_____

_____

_____

_____

DETECTIVE'S DESK #3

THE CASE OF
The Closed Curtain

"Go, Sherlock," screamed Sheila as her brother kicked the soccer ball into the net for a goal. All along her side of the field people cheered.

Suddenly everyone got very quiet. Something was wrong on the field. The players and the coaches clustered at one end. Sheila stared hard trying to find Sherlock.

"Sherlock's hurt," yelled a spectator.

Sheila gasped.

???

"Tell me it's not possible," said Sherlock as he lay on the table in the emergency room.

"It's not possible," said Sheila.

"But it is," said Sherlock. "I broke my ankle and I'm going to miss the playoff game on Saturday."

A nurse came. "Now the cast is all set and we can take you to your room," he said to Sherlock.

Sheila trotted to keep up with the moving table that carried Sherlock as it rolled down the hallway. The nurse pushed it through swinging doors. On one door was a sign: "NO CHILDREN UNDER 18 ADMITTED."

Sheila ignored the sign and kept going but the table stopped.

"Say, 'goodbye,'" said the nurse, pointing at the sign.

"Goodbye, Sherlock," said Sheila. "I'll write you right away."

Sherlock waved and then disappeared as the doors closed behind him.

???

A nurse took the thermometer out of Sherlock's mouth.

"Why is the curtain around the other bed closed?" asked Sherlock.

"Your temperature is normal," said the nurse. "Drink lots of water," and she was gone.

Two game shows and one soap opera later a doctor rushed by Sherlock's bed with a newspaper under her arm. She went behind the curtain around the next bed but was only in there for a few moments. Sherlock looked away from the TV high on the wall across from his bed as the doctor left. "Hey," said Sherlock, "you forgot your newspaper." But she went out the door without noticing. Sherlock looked back up at the TV.

Halfway through an old cowboy movie, a woman dressed in pink and white stripes came in. "For you," she said and handed Sherlock an envelope.

It had no return address, but he recognized Sheila's writing and tore the envelope open:

Dear Sherlock,
I'm sorry your ankle broke and you have to miss the game. I wish I could visit you. I have an idea. ⊙ U read this? since U R probably ▭▭ U ⊙-u U write me in rebuses, like this.

I'll write you back in words because I'm busy as a bee and you're not.
Love,
Sheila

Sherlock was tired of TV already so he started a letter to Sheila right away:

> Dear Sheila,
> [eye] [can]t [stop] th+[ink]+ing about the boy
> in the next [bed]. [eye] [can]t [H+P]
> & he doesn't eat NE food. Could
> [foot]+-L [bug] in a coma? 2+ day
> 6 doctors & 8 nurses came 2 C him.
> Love,
> Sher+[lock]

Sherlock sent this letter to Sheila with his parents when they visited him that evening. The next day they brought him this reply:

> Dear Sherlock,
> This is hot stuff. A mystery right in your own hospital room! You sure are lucky. But why don't you peek in and see?
> Love,
> Sheila

He wrote back:

> Dear Sheila,
> [eye] [can]t look. It's not po+[ear]: [H+P],
> is what [eye]ve Cn.
>
> [foot]+-L doesn't get NE food or dr+[ink].
> [eye] [can]t [H+P] NE thing. No 1
> comes 2 C him. No [car]+ds or [flowers]. The
> cur+[ten] is never O+[pen].

???

When Sheila got that letter she called Sherlock on the phone in his room.

"Hi," she said.

"Sheila? Why are you calling? How can I send you a rebus on the phone?"

"I'm much too curious to wait for a letter now," she said. "Tell me, Sherlock, does anybody ever take any bottles of liquid behind that curtain?"

"No, never."

"Then you can go look. I'm sure that there isn't anybody behind that curtain. You can live without food, but you have to have water."

"You want me to look right now?"

"Yes. I'm dying of curiosity."

Sherlock went over to the curtain. He parted it a little bit and peeked in carefully just in case Sheila was wrong. She wasn't. He opened it all the way and took a good look. Then he went back to the phone.

"You were right, Sheila. Nobody in there."

"Come on Sherlock, what was in there? Don't keep me in suspense."

Sherlock was tempted to tease her a little, but she'd been so nice to him since he hurt his ankle that he told her right away. "There's just a newspaper on a table open to the crossword puzzle. Most of the words are filled in. That's what all those doctors and nurses do in there—the crossword."

???

"Well, you've been here too long, Sherlock," said Dr. Blackwell. "I'm sending you home today. See you in my office next week."

The doctor looked at his watch then he slipped through the curtain by the other bed. Sherlock shouted to him, "I think two down is 'apple.'"

Dr. Blackwell came out. "Right you are, Sherlock." He winked.

Sherlock winked back.

THE END

Haiku, Can You?

A bush warbler comes
Wiping his mud-covered feet
On the plum blossoms.

This poem is a haiku. That's a kind of Japanese poem. Haiku **don't** rhyme but they **are** supposed to have a certain number of sounds (syllables)—five in the first line, seven in the second, five in the third. **Like this:**

RAINWORK
Raindrops fall slowly (5)
Wetting the dusty sidewalk. (7)
I don't like homework. (5)

Many Haiku sound strange because they have a last line that seems to have nothing to do with the other two lines (like the haiku above, *Rainwork).*
But, in haiku, the last lines really do have **some** connection with the other two lines. It's just sometimes hard to figure out what the connection is. If you think about it long enough you can probably come up with a connection for the last line of *Rainwork*—maybe the writer was sitting inside watching the rain and wanting to go out and play instead of doing homework? Maybe the writer hates rain the same way she hates homework?

Because the last line often doesn't **seem** to have anything to do with the first two it can be a lot of fun to write last lines for haiku.

Try these:

A twig is broken,
A rabbit hops through the woods.

_____

The wooden bridge creaks
As I walk across the stream.

_____

The butterfly cleans
Its feet in the petal's dew.

_____ •

My blue jeans are clean
And the summer sun is bright

_____ •

The smell of cookies
Baking in the kitchen stove

_____ •

Hot tar on the street
Smells like summer and no school

_____ •

Big grows my balloon
As I blow and blow and blow.

_____ •

Jets take off loudly
While birds flap their wings to fly

_____ •

The winter frost hangs
Icicles from my house

_____ •

I imagine things
Spaceships and kings and horses

_____ •

The tree in my yard,
Full of chattering squirrels

_____ •

The leaves in autumn
Watch each other as they fall

_____ •

Jet planes leave high trails
Crisscrossing the cloudy sky

_____ •

Try writing your own haiku. It's fun.

A Picture is Worth a Word

What if you couldn't write and you wanted to send a message about a house. What would you do?

Easy. I'd draw a picture of a house, like this. ⌂

What if you wanted to send a message about a man?

I'd draw a picture of a man, like this. ⚲

What if you wanted to say "run fast"?

That's not so easy. I could use feet like this ⫘⫘ **for run, but I'd have to make up a picture for "fast," something like this** ⟹ **but maybe no one else would understand.**

This kind of writing, writing with pictures, is called **pictographic** writing and lots of people, like American Indians and Egyptians, used writing like this. It was easier for them because they agreed with each other on what the pictures meant. That way, if a Kiowa Indian wanted to say "fear" he would draw 〰 and he'd know other Kiowa Indians would understand.

Here's a pictographic language we invented. Use it to translate the message below.

Future (This symbol can make words talk about the future. It can make "is" into "will be.") $>$

Past (This symbol can make words talk about the past. It can make "is" into "was.") $<$

Question (This symbol can turn a word into a question. It can make "you do" into "do you?") $?$

I, me (One symbol can mean both of these.) $\circ$

is, am, are (One symbol can mean all of these.) $\times$

fun

house

like

message

write

you

end of sentence

end of message

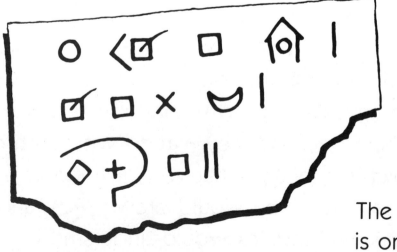

The translation is on page 115.

Now you can make up your own pictographic language with a friend and use it to write each other messages. When you do a pictographic message it's easier if you leave out words like "the" and "a" and other words that you don't need in order to understand the message.

Here is a list of words for you to use to make up your own pictographic language. Add more words to these whenever you want.

Future (This symbol can make words talk about the future. It can make "is" into "will be.") _____

Past (This symbol can make words talk about the past. It can make "is" into "was.") _____

Question (This symbol can turn a word into a question. It can make "you do" into "do you?") _____

I, me (One symbol can mean both of these.) _____

is, am, are (One symbol can mean all of these.) _____

My friends (Put their names on the left and the symbol in the blank.)

_____   _____

_____   _____

_____   _____

_____   _____

_____   _____

_____   _____

_____   _____

ball	_____	in	_____	
bike	_____	like		
call	_____	lunch	_____	
cloudy	_____	meet	_____	
club	_____	meeting	_____	
come	_____	message	_____	
day	_____	phone	_____	
today	_____	play	_____	
tomorrow	_____	run	_____	
yesterday	_____	sad	_____	
hour	_____	school	_____	
A.M. (morning)	_____	sunny	_____	
P.M. (afternoon)	_____	teacher	_____	
Monday	_____	toy	_____	
Tuesday	_____	TV	_____	
Wednesday	_____	walk	_____	
Thursday	_____	watch	_____	
Friday	_____	write	_____	
Saturday	_____	yesterday	_____	
Sunday	_____	you	_____	
eat	_____	end of sentence	_____	
fun	_____	end of message	_____	
game	_____	relatives:		
go	_____	mother	_____	
happy	_____	father	_____	
house	_____	my sister	_____	
homework	_____	my brother	_____	

sisters & brothers _____

(Put their names in these spaces.)

Add your own words in the blanks here as you need them.

_____ _____ _____ _____

_____ _____ _____ _____

_____ _____ _____ _____

_____ _____ _____ _____

_____ _____ _____ _____

_____ _____ _____ _____

When you make up your own messages, you can always write out a word if you haven't put it in your dictionary yet or if it's a word that you don't often use.

Here's some space for your first pictogram message!

Story Starter #5:
THE OLD HOUSE

The stairs creaked as we climbed toward the landing. The moon was bright enough to see the broken stairs but it was still a scary place to be at night. Then we heard an eerie noise from the second floor . . . .
(What was the noise? Where were you?
And what happened next?
Finish the story.)

THE CASE OF
The Smiling Symbol

"She'd better get here soon," said Sheila, kicking a pebble across her driveway. "I have to get information for the Case of the Aggravating Aardvark and the library closes in less than an hour."

"Who is *she* and what is the Case of the Aggravating Aardvark?" asked Sherlock, Sheila's younger brother. But a girl dressed in a yellow T-shirt and blue jeans skidded her bike to a stop in front of Sheila before she could answer.

"Hi, Susan," said Sheila, "I've been waiting for you."

A brown and white beagle ran up behind Susan. "Come on, Africa," shouted Susan.

"Africa?" said Sherlock.

"His real name is Spot but my best friend, Molly, calls him 'Africa' because that big brown blotch on his back looks like Africa."

Sherlock examined the dog's back. "She's right, It's Africa all right."

"Well, we have a geography test on Monday. Does Molly borrow Africa to study?" asked Sheila, laughing at her own joke.

"I thought you told me that your geography tests are so easy that nobody studies for them," said Sherlock.

"Nobody but Molly," said Susan. "She studies all day before any test. She is a very serious student."

"Weird," said Sherlock. "Hey, Sheila, tell me about the Aggravating Aardvark Case."

Sheila ignored Sherlock. "Susan, you said you needed our help."

"I'm desperate. I've got to let my dad know by tonight which day I can go and Molly's not home and—"

"Susan," Sheila interrupted, "start at the beginning."

"Well, Molly and I made up our own secret picture language. We send each other messages in pictograms. Today she stuck a message in my notebook. But when I got home to read it I couldn't figure out one of the symbols."

"Why don't you call up Molly and ask her?" asked Sheila.

"She won't be home until tomorrow morning."

"Susan," Sherlock cut in, "do you know anything about the Case of the Aggravating Aardvark?"

Before Susan could answer Sherlock, Sheila said, "Let me see the note."

This is what Susan handed Sheila:

"How much of it do you understand?" asked Sheila.

"Everything but the circle with two smiles in it. The black-eyed Susan means me, Susan. Dark curly hair is Molly. The two arrows meeting means 'meet' and the wedge pointing right makes it 'will meet.' The house is a house and because it has the Molly symbol in it, it means her house. So I know that up to there the note says, 'Susan, I will meet you at my house.'" She looked at the note and bit her lip, then went on, "Circles are for different days and the three dots on the right makes it three o'clock in the afternoon. But I don't know the day. The circle with two smiles is either Saturday or Sunday, I don't know which, and I have to know to tell my father when I can go to the circus with him."

"Didn't you make a dictionary of all your words and symbols so you'd remember them?" asked Sherlock.

Susan pulled some ragged and faded pieces of paper from her pocket. "Sure we did, but I left it in my pocket when my jeans were washed and now there are parts I can't read anymore, like the symbols for Saturday and Sunday. One of them is a circle with one smile and the other's a circle with two, and I can't remember which is which. That's the whole problem."

"I have the solution," said Sherlock.

"What is it?" asked Sheila.

"First you tell me about the Aggravating Aardvark Case, Sheila."

"Come on Sherlock, just tell us." His sister was annoyed.

Sherlock picked up a stick and threw it across the front lawn. Dr. Watson (their dog) and Africa raced after it.

"Sherlock!" snapped Sheila.

"Okay, okay. If the circle has two smiles it's got to be Saturday."

"Why?" Sheila and Susan both asked.

"Because Saturday is better than Sunday."

The two dogs ran back, both without the stick.

"That's what you think," said Susan, "but I like Sunday better. That's the problem. Molly likes Saturday better, like you, Sherlock, but I like Sunday better and I can't remember which of us got to choose."

"I guess this doesn't have such an easy solution," said Sherlock.

"It's hopeless," said Susan. Sherlock looked at Sheila. She was sitting cross-legged on the porch. "She's thinking," said Sherlock.

Africa trotted over to Sheila for a pat. His head went under Sheila's hand and bounced it up so it would fall on his head.

"I've got it!" said Sheila. "Saturday. Two smiles in a circle means Saturday."

"You mean I was right?" asked Sherlock.

"Yes," said Sheila, "but only by accident."

"Thanks a lot," said Susan. "Now I've got to go."

"Don't you want to know how I solved the case?" asked Sheila.

"Oh, yes. But tell me quick, I've got to get to the library."

"Well, I got the clue when Africa made me pet him. The blotch on Africa's back reminded me about our test on Monday. You told me that Molly always studies all day before any test so she'll be studying on Sunday. So she must have invited you over for Saturday."

"That's great, Sheila," said Susan, as she straddled her bike.

"Wait," said Sheila, "I'll ride with you. I'm going to the library, too."

Sheila got on her bike. As she and Susan rolled down the driveway Sherlock called, "Are you researching aggravating aardvarks, too, Susan?"

She stopped her bike and looked at him in surprise. "How did you know that, Sherlock? We have to do a composition about aardvarks for school and it's pretty aggravating."

Sheila and Susan rode off down the street with Africa running behind. Sherlock ran into the road and shouted after Sheila, "That's not a case, Sheila. You can't call that a case, Sheila. It's not a case." Dr. Watson (their dog) stood next to him barking.

THE END

Now try drawing your own cartoon adventure

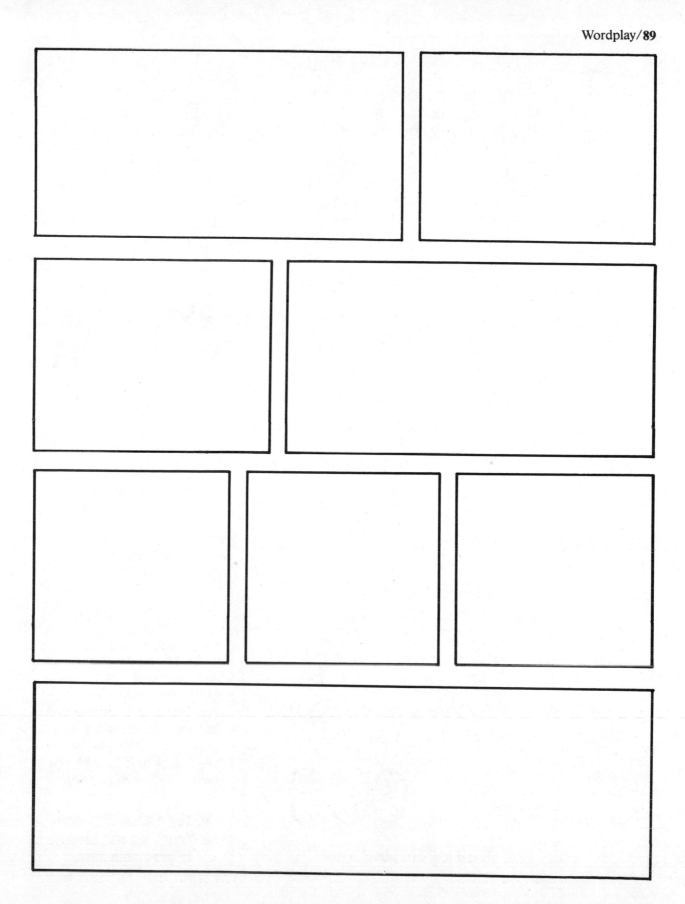

Funny Ads

Advertising can be funny and it's fun to make up your own ads (like we've done on this page). On the next two pages, we've invented products and written "copy" (information about the product) for some ads. All you have to do is draw a picture of the product.

The Truth About Advertising

Advertising can be fun, but it can also be serious business. There are grown-ups who do nothing else when they're working but make up advertisements. There's a good reason for this. If there weren't advertising you wouldn't know that there was a great new movie playing downtown or that a new record by your favorite group had come out. And if there weren't any advertising you wouldn't know that they'd invented a new flavor of ice cream or a faster bicycle.

But sometimes advertising gets a little silly. You know that just because they've invented an electric gizmo for filing your fingernails doesn't mean your friends won't like you if you don't file your fingernails electrically. And you definitely know that just because some billboards make cigarettes look cool or grown-up doesn't mean that it's cool or grown-up to smoke cigarettes. (It's not, it's stupid.)

Creating products and advertisements can be fun. We've provided plenty pf space to do both on the next three pages.

So pick a funny product and get into the advertising business!

Introducing
BRUSH-NO-MORE GUM

Say goodbye to toothbrushing and dentists forever!

Now, toothbrushing is forever obsolete. Dentists may as well retire. Here's a new kind of gum, opposed by the American Dental Association, that does everything toothbrushing does... and more.

It prevents cavities, removes food particles and plaque, whitens your teeth, and freshens your breath.

You'll never have to brush your teeth or visit a dentist again.

So buy a pack of "Brush-No-More" and say goodbye to your toothbrush.

The Multicycle—Everything You Need in a Bicycle and More

Next time you ride a bike, ride a Multicycle. It has more wheels to make you go faster, more handlebars to make you steer better, and more seats to give you the most comfortable ride you've ever had.

Ride the Multicycle and see!

We've given you the product ideas— now you write the ad!

SWEET DREAM
PILLOW

Pet-A-Day Club

"Sick-All-Over" Cream

SMART PENCIL

Here are some more ideas that need ads!

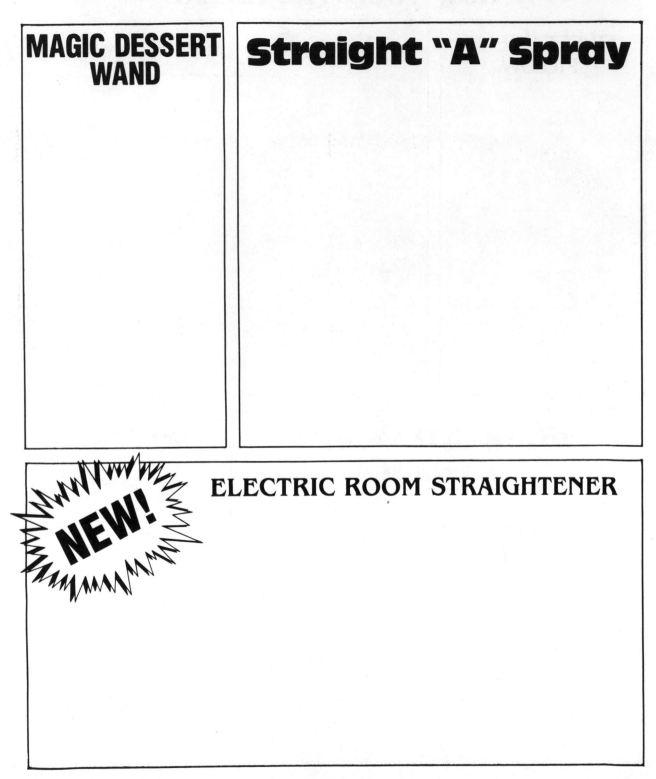

MAGIC DESSERT WAND

Straight "A" Spray

NEW!

ELECTRIC ROOM STRAIGHTENER

Here is some space for you to make up your own ads for funny products!

DOING CROSSWORDS

The first part of doing crosswords is guessing words. Sometimes that's easy:

1. What's a three-letter word for a big monkey?

_____ _____ _____

(Hint: King Kong is not the answer.)

2. A four-letter thing that carries people in the water:

_____ _____ _____ _____

(Not a rock).

In a crossword they don't tell you how many letters are in the word. You find that out by counting boxes.

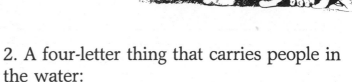

NOT THAT KIND OF BOXES!

This kind of boxes:

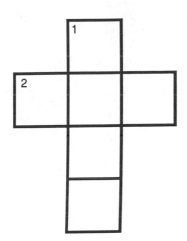

Number 1 Down has four letters and 2 Across has three.

Here are the clues:

Across
2. Opposite of young.

Down
1. Color.

Here's a bigger one

(Answers are on page 116)

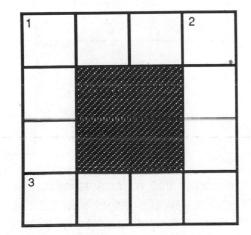

Across
1. Sometimes it rhymes.
3. If you take one we hope you get an "A."

Down
1. What dogs do when they're hot.
2. Hamburgers and hot dogs are made of this.

And that's all there is to it. The more you do, the better you get. **Try these:**

Puzzle #1

Across

1. A noisy sip.
4. Opposite of younger.
5. The kind of bird that catches the worm. (Not a late bird.)

Down

1. A sleeping noise some people make.
2. Opposite of over.
3. When you're invited to one you probably get cake and ice cream.

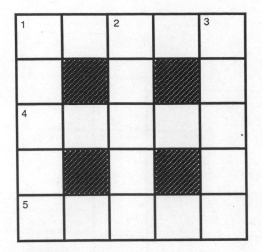

Puzzle #2

Across

1. You pick things up (and drop them) with one of these, and you only have two.
3. One of these is probably inside your shoe.
5. You can do this on ice, but it's not as much fun as skating.
6. I'd rather be first (or even second, third, fourth, or fifth) than this.
8. A stumble or a journey. (I'd prefer a journey.)
9. I have ten of these in my shoes.

Down

1. They lay those oval white things we eat for breakfast. (I forget what they're called.)
2. If I did this to my mother's fancy china vase, it would break all over the floor and she'd be unhappy about it, so I hold on to it tight.
3. You close your hand to make one, but don't punch anybody with it.

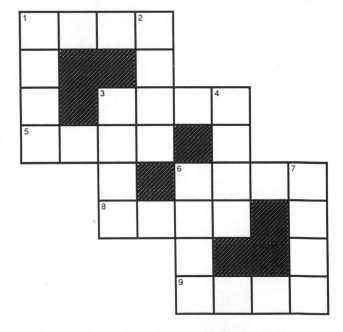

4. Something to catch animals with (though they would rather you didn't).
6. If I do this to something heavy, it hurts my back, but I try not to drop it on my toe.
7. If bottoms are on one end, then these are on the other.

Puzzle #3

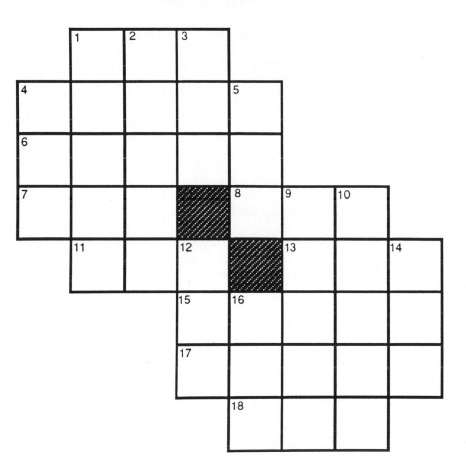

Across

1. A big lake or a little ocean.
4. Form.
6. Can't wait; a kind of beaver.
7. The whole thing; opposite of nothing.
8. Went fast. (If you did this in the corridor in school you might have gotten in trouble.)
11. Connects your hip to your ankle.
13. A negative ("no") word.
15. Nickname for Anne or Ann but not for Zachary.
17. If your shoelace is this, you might trip on it.
18. You can color cloth or hair with this (or maybe the sofa, but probably not the car).

Down

1. Will.
2. The bird on quarters. (Some of them are bald.)
3. Big monkey. (Still not King Kong.)
4. Little ocean or a big lake. (Sound familiar?)
5. To make a mistake. (Even you must do it sometimes.)
9. Bother or pester. (Sometimes I do it to my big sister.)
10. Sound. Too much of this is a good way to do the last clue (#9).
12. Slang for girl.
14. A summertime kind of shirt.
16. A quiet way to say yes.

Puzzle #4

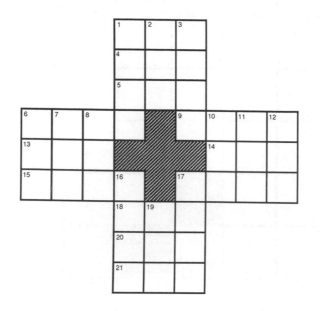

Across

1. Finger painting and the Mona Lisa are different kinds of this.
4. If I hold an aardvark or anything in front of your eyes this is what they do to it. (It's what your eyes do all the time.)
5. Female name.
6. A fish you'll meet more often on sandwiches than in the water.
9. A female papa.
13. Do something with.
14. Brother of a lass.
15. Flying rodents or things you hit baseballs with (but don't try hitting baseballs with flying rodents).
17. Mountains in Switzerland.
18. A game in which one person runs after everybody else until they catch somebody or until suppertime.
20. The stuff you fall on when you ice skate.
21. The color of apples, stop lights, and the crayon I lost last week.

Down

1. China's continent (not Greenland).
2. Color of my favorite shirt (and 21 Across).
3. A group that plays on the same side in a game of baseball or basketball (or tiddlywinks).
6. If you don't like baths don't get into this.
7. Initials of a country, the home of Abraham Lincoln, George Washington, and me.
8. You can catch butterflies with one or hit tennis balls over one (but don't use the same one).
10. The whole thing, every little bitty bit of it.
11. Paper that helps you find your way. (Better still, don't get lost.)
12. Puts two and two together to get (we hope) four.
16. Mix with a spoon (not with a pencil).
17. Got old.
19. Number one playing card.

Puzzle #5

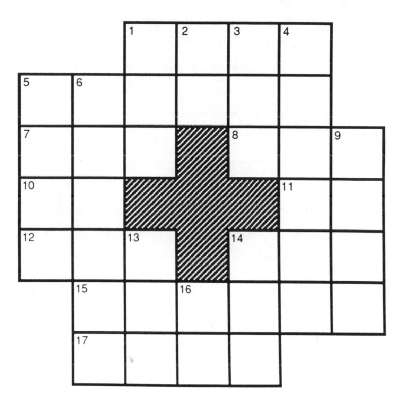

Across

1. A very little bit.
5. If you make these people will cover their ears.
7. Not young.
8. The highest playing card.
10. What you do to seven and three to get ten. (If you subtract, you're in trouble.)
11. Nickname for Alan (or Algernon or Albert, for that matter).
12. Bottom of a skirt or dress.
14. Opposite of downs. (Did you ever hear of a plural of down before this? Isn't that ridiculous?)
15. Teeter-totter, only backwards. (Even more ridiculous than 14 Across.)
17. Big thing with leaves. (Definitely not King Kong holding a bush.)

Down

1. Short for middle.
2. The opposite of isn't (and not un-isn't or anti-isn't).
3. A hot drink made with a bag. (The idea of drinking a wet bag is pretty yucky to me.)
4. Get away, break out of jail, sneak out of your room when you should be doing homework.
5. Made the Ark.
6. Older than old, even older than older.
9. Something different is "something _____."
13. Scratch or damage. (Don't do this to your aunt's best table top.)
14. Do something with.
16. You and I.

Puzzle #6

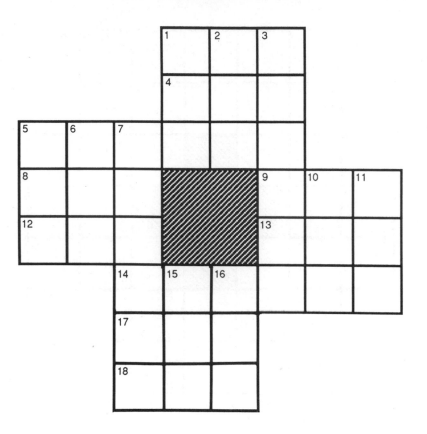

Across

1. The thing a cow says most (definitely not "yup" or "hi").
4. Your hand is at the end of one.
5. Slang for a small person.
8. Woman's name.
9. Place to park many cars.
12. Opposite of "no." (Isn't that a ridiculously easy clue?)
13. Female sheep. (Definitely not an easy clue, but you had your chance with #12.)
14. Tell on someone. (Don't do it to me. Please.)
17. Pirates may wear a patch over one.
18. The color of raspberries, strawberries, and ketchup. (Not a tasty dish all together.)

Down

1. Female paw, slang for mother.
2. Metal when it's mined.
3. A dish made of eggs.
5. Give money for something.
6. Night before; Adam's best and only friend.
7. When the bunny brings candy and eggs in a basket.
10. Night bird that goes "Whoooo."
11. What you put a golf ball on before you hit it.
15. Opposite of "nay," a way sailors say "yes."
16. Nickname for Theodore.

MAKE YOUR OWN CROSSWORDS

I had the best time making up the clues to the crosswords in the Crossword chapter. There's no reason why you shouldn't have the same fun.

A clue for the word "school" could be:

A place where children learn.

or it could be:

A group of fish.

or it could be a little tricky, like this:

The place where I spend most of my days.

It's up to you how you define the word. That's what makes it fun.

Here are some crossword solutions. But the words need definitions. After each crossword box there's a place for you to write definitions for the words in the box.

Across

3. (APPLE)

_____

4. (TRICK)

_____

Down

1. (SPARE)

_____

2. (SLICE)

_____

Across

3. (DOCTOR)

_____

4. (HEDGES)

_____

_____

Down

1. (HOUSES)

_____

2. (COBWEB)

_____

Across

1. (STAMP)

_____

4. (ABOVE)

_____

5. (EDGES)

_____

_____

Down

1. (SHAVE)

_____

2. (ALONG)

_____

3. (POEMS)

_____

_____

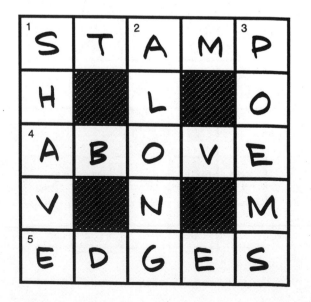

Across

2. (FINGER)

_____

_____

5. (BIGGEST)

_____

_____

6. (TATTLE)

_____

_____

Down

1. (AFRICA)

_____

_____

3. (NIGHT)

_____

_____

4. (EASIER)

_____

_____

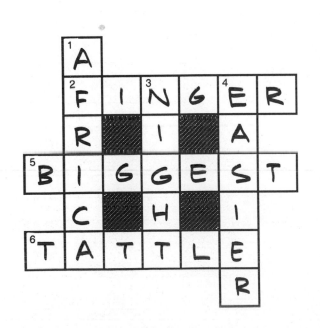

Across

3. (COMPANY)

_____

_____

5. (SANTA)

_____

_____

6. (BEHAVED)

_____

_____

Down

1. (TOASTER)

_____

_____

2. (SNEAKER)

_____

_____

4. (PANDA)

_____

_____

Of course, the making-up-clues part is only one part of making up whole crossword puzzles. The rest is fun, too.

First, you make a crossword box and find words that fit. Try different words. Sometimes you have to try a lot of different words before you get one that fits (so make sure you use a pencil and an eraser), but when you get it you feel great.

Try fitting words into these boxes for practice. **Be sure you use a pencil!**

After you've fit words into these boxes, you can make up definitions for them in the blanks on the right.

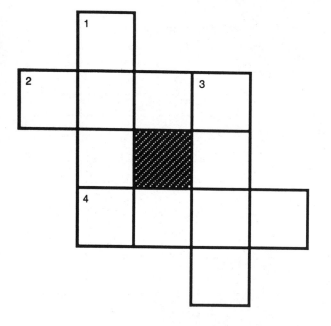

Across

_____

_____

_____

_____

_____

Down

_____

_____

_____

_____

_____

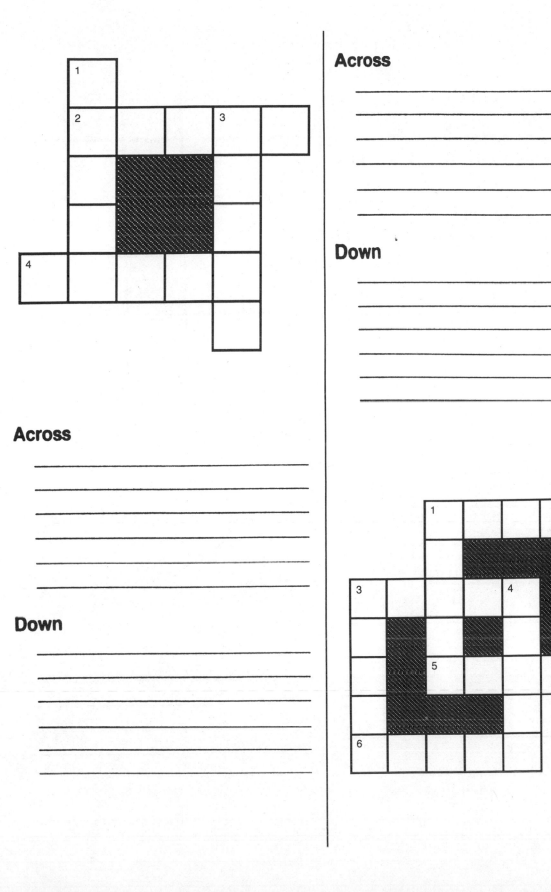

Across

_____

_____

_____

_____

_____

_____

Down

_____

_____

_____

_____

_____

_____

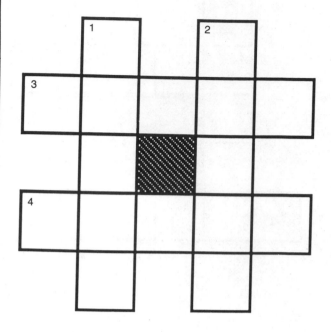

Across

_____

_____

_____

_____

_____

_____

Down

_____

_____

_____

_____

_____

_____

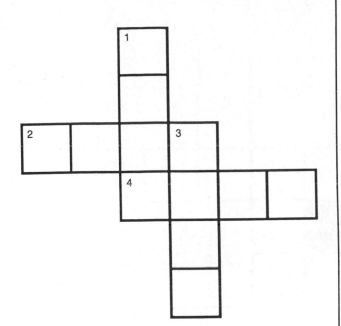

Across

_____

_____

_____

_____

_____

Down

_____

_____

_____

_____

_____

_____

Across

_____

_____

_____

_____

_____

Down

_____

_____

_____

_____

_____

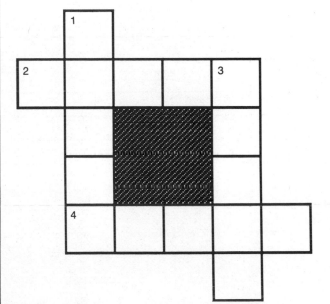

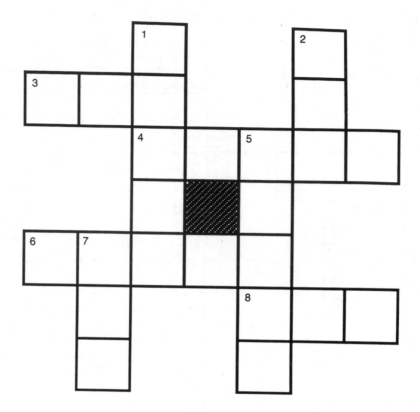

Across

_____
_____
_____
_____
_____
_____
_____
_____

Down

_____
_____
_____
_____
_____
_____
_____
_____

Across

_____
_____
_____
_____
_____
_____
_____

Down

_____
_____
_____
_____
_____
_____
_____

Now try making your own crosswords

Across

_____
_____
_____
_____
_____
_____
_____
_____

Down

_____
_____
_____
_____
_____
_____
_____
_____

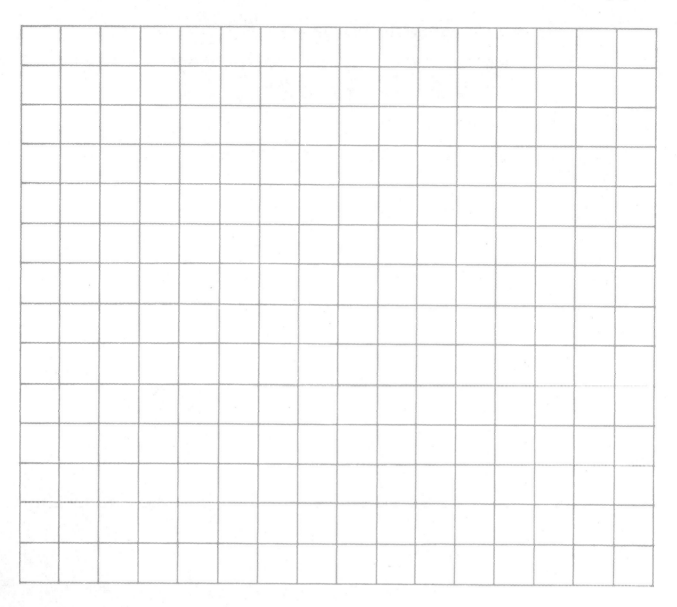

Across

_____

_____

_____

_____

_____

_____

_____

_____

Down

_____

_____

_____

_____

_____

_____

_____

_____

Story Starter #7:
THE GIANT

He was sleeping in the grass in a field when I found him. At first I was scared because he was taller than my house. He must have heard me creeping away because he woke up and gave me such a warm smile that I liked him right away.

"Are you a friend?" he asked. His voice was very loud.

"What do you mean?" I said.

"I need a friend," he said and he started to look sad.

(What did you say? And what happened then? Finish the story.)

Hinky Pinkies Solutions:

(page 2)

1. jolly holly
2. brown gown
3. cheap sheep
4. ocean motion
5. bees' knees
6. Mike's bikes
7. star car
8. pop top
9. lead bread
10. carriage marriage

11. cellar yeller
12. ghost post
13. trash rash
14. phony pony
15. sandy candy
16. happy pappy
17. gag bag
18. damp lamp
19. rug bug
20. rocket locket

21. couch grouch
22. boys' toys
23. Coke joke
24. belly jelly
25. chilly Billy
26. ants' pants
27. wing ring
28. mouse house
29. road toad
30. snake cake

Solution to the Case of the Science Class Code message:
(page 18)

CANYOUSTAYOVERATMYHOUSETONIGHTTELLMEATSOCCERPRACTICETODAY

CAN YOU STAY OVER AT MY HOUSE TONIGHT? TELL ME AT SOCCER PRACTICE TODAY.

Solution to the Case of the Keyless Code message:
(page 39)

DEAR WILLIAM,
    I'M GLAD YOU FOUND THE
KEY WRITTEN INSIDE THE
ENVELOPE. I'M ALSO GLAD
YOU FOUND YOUR BIKE.
LET'S GO FOR A BIKE RIDE
NEXT SATURDAY.
                    YOUR FRIEND,
                    THOMAS

Solutions to HERE TO THERE
(page 48)

JOLLY	PRANK	WORMS	PAPER
holly	plank	warms	piper
hilly	blank	warts	pipes
hills	bland	darts	piles
hilts	blend	dares	files
HINTS	**BLEED**	**DARED**	**FILMS**

DRINK	PLANT	FLOCK	BIKER
drank	plane	block	baker
prank	plank	black	bakes
plank	blank	blank	bases
plane	blink	bland	basks
PLATE	**BRINK**	**BRAND**	**TASKS**

A Picture is Worth a Word
(page 76)

TRANSLATION [The words in parentheses like (this) are words that we left out of the message]:

I wrote (this) message in my house. Write (ing) (this) message is fun. Do you like (this) message?

Solutions to Doing Crosswords
(Page 94)

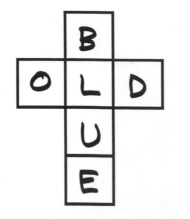

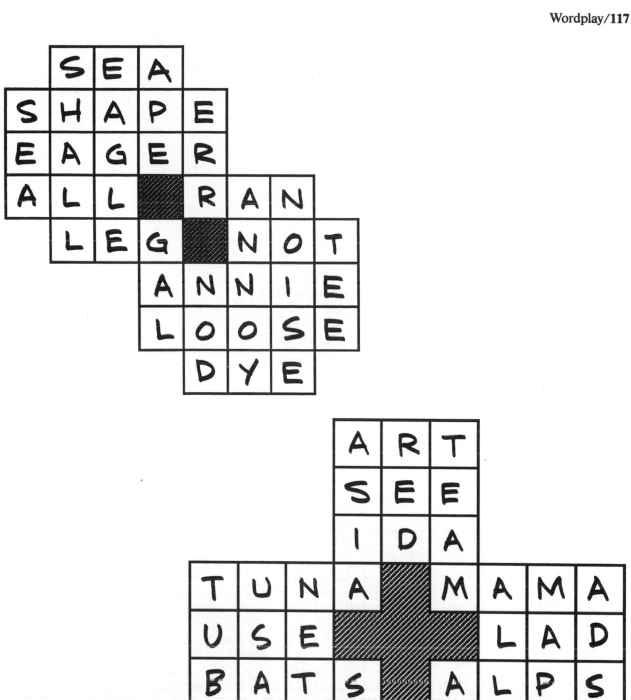

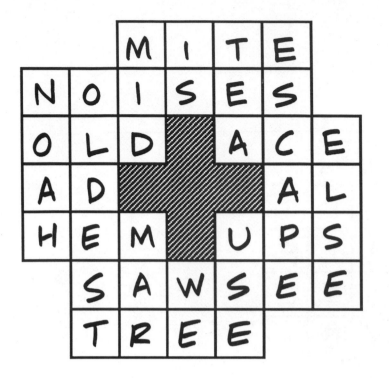

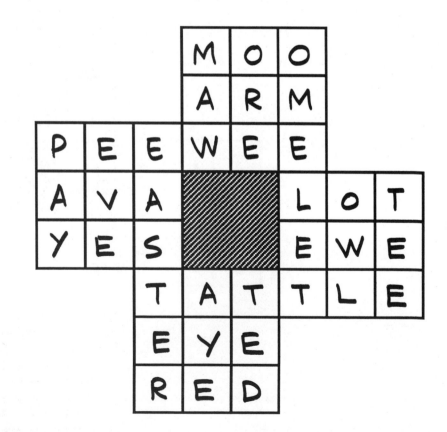

Free Stuff For Kids (10th ed.)
by the Free Stuff Editors

One of the all-time best-selling children's activity books, this book is a catalog of free and up-to-two-dollar things kids can send for by mail, such as posters, bumper stickers, coloring books, comics, stickers, decals, and more.
(S&S Ordering Number 63066-0) $3.95

The "Solve-it-Yourself" Mystery Series...

Volume #2
The Case of the Chocolate Snatcher
A masked thief makes off with a fortune in chocolates. Hawkeye, Amy and Sgt. Treadwell track down three tough suspects, and Hawkeye's sketch pins the guilt on one—can you tell who did it? Eight other cases, too.
(S&S Ordering Number 54472-1) $1.95

Volume #7
The Mystery of the "Star Ship" Movie
Hawkeye and Amy are visiting a movie set when a man snatches a copy of a new film and dashes off. He's hiding somewhere among the robots and space ships—but Hawkeye's sketch shows where he is. Can you find him? Plus eight other cases.
(S&S Ordering Number 54483-7) $1.95

Volume #8
The Secret of the Software Spy
Hawkeye and Amy have to spot a computer software spy who just stole an important program. He is supposed to be eating at a fancy restaurant. A sketch tips them off—and you, too. Plus eight other mysteries.
(S&S Ordering Number 54491-8) $1.95

Volume #9
The Case of the Toilet Paper Decorator

A storm wipes out the power in Lakewood Hills, and that same night, someone TPs Mr. Bronson's house. Who's the culprit? The two suspects seem to have good stories—but Hawkeye's sketch gives one away. Plus eight other cases.
(S&S Ordering Number 54479-9) $1.95

Volume #10
The Secret of the Loon Lake Monster

There's a monster in Loon Lake—everybody's looking for it! One man has a photo of it, but when Hawkeye and Amy see it, they smell a fish right away. Can you see why it's a fake? Try
(S&S Ordering Number 54490-X) $1.95

Volume #12
The Secret of the Video Game Scores

Amy's rated #2 at the Crazy Caterpillar video game, and her #7-ranked cousin, Toni, is upset. Then Toni gets mysteriously ill—but when Hawkeye shows Amy a sketch of the ratings, all mysteries are over. Nine other cases, too.
(S&S Ordering Number 54466-7) $1.95

Volume #13
The Mystery of the Phony Frankenstein

A purse snatching interrupts Hawkeye, Amy and Sergeant Treadwell's trip to a horror movie. Their investigation turns up two freaky Frankenstein monsters. One is a fake—and the culprit.
(S&S Ordering Number 55615-0) $2.50

Volume #14
The Case of the Clever Marathon Cheat

Hawkeye and Amy have front-row seats at the L.A. Olympics track and field events. It's Amy's chance photo of a marathon contestant that helps crack the case when the long shot competitor ends up winning.
(S&S Ordering Number 55614-2) $2.50

ORDER FORM

____63066-0	Free Stuff For Kids	............................$3.95
____63099-7	Wordplay	....................................$4.95
____54472-1 (Vol. 2)	The Case of the Chocolate Snatcher	..............$1.95
____54488-8 (Vol. 5)	The Case of the Clever Computer Crooks	.......$1.95
____54483-7 (Vol. 7)	The Mystery of the "Star Ship" Movie	..........$1.95
____54491-8 (Vol. 9)	The Case of the Toilet Paper Decorator	........$1.95
____54490-X (Vol. 10)	The Case of the Loon Lake Monster	............$1.95
____54465-9 (Vol. 11)	The Mystery of the Haunted House	..............$1.95
____54466-7 (Vol. 12)	The Secret of the Video Game Scores	...........$1.95
____55615-0 (Vol. 13)	The Mystery of the Phony Frankenstein	.........$2.50
____55614-2 (Vol. 14)	The Case of the Clever Marathon Cheat	........$2.50

Please send me copies of the books checked above. I am enclosing $_____ which covers the full amount per book shown above plus $1.00 for postage and handling for the first book and $.50 for each additional book. (Add $2.00 to total for postage and handling for books shipped to Canada. Overseas postage and handling will be billed. MN residents add 6% sales tax.) Allow up to four weeks for delivery. Quantity discounts available upon request.

Send check or money order to Meadowbrook, Inc. No cash or C.O.D.s, please.

For purchases over $10.00, you may use VISA or MasterCard (order by mail or phone). For these orders we need information below. Charge to: ☐ VISA ☐ MasterCard

Account # _____

Expiration Date _____

Card Signature _____

Send book(s) to:

Name _____

Address _____

City _____ State _____ Zip _____

Mail order to: Book Orders, Meadowbrook, Inc., 18318 Minnetonka Blvd., Deephaven, MN 55391, Phone Orders: (612) 473-5400